I0203409

Free Verse Editions
Edited by Jon Thompson

erros

Morgan Lucas Schuldt

Parlor Press
Anderson, South Carolina
www.parlorpress.com

Parlor Press LLC, Anderson, South Carolina, 29621

© 2013 by Parlor Press
All rights reserved.
Printed in the United States of America
S A N: 2 5 4 - 8 8 7 9

Library of Congress Cataloging-in-Publication Data

Schuldt, Morgan Lucas.
    [Poems. Selections]
    Erros / Morgan Lucas Schuldt.
        pages cm. -- (Free Verse Editions)
    Includes bibliographical references and index.
    ISBN 978-1-60235-376-3 (paperback : acid-free paper) -- ISBN 978-1-
60235-377-0 (Adobe ebook) -- ISBN 978-1-60235-378-7 (ePub)
    I. Rickel, Boyer. II. Title.
    PS3619.C47E77 2013
    811'.6--dc23
                                        2013019919

1 2 3 4 5

Cover design by Boyer Rickel and Gary Kautto.
Author Photo: Barbara Cully

Printed on acid-free paper.

Parlor Press, LLC is an independent publisher of scholarly and trade
titles in print and multimedia formats. This book is available in
paperback and ebook formats from Parlor Press on the World Wide Web
at http://www.parlorpress.com or through online and brick-and-mortar
bookstores. For submission information or to find out about Parlor Press
publications, write to Parlor Press, 3015 Brackenberry Drive, Anderson,
South Carolina, 29621, or email editor@parlorpress.com.

for my parents

Contents

Foreword

Morgan Lucas Schuldt died on Jan. 30, 2012, twelve days before his thirty-fourth birthday, at the conclusion of a double-lung transplant. A few months before, in early fall as he waited on oxygen for appropriate lungs, Morgan finalized and emailed me his second book-length manuscript, *Erros*, asking that, "should something happen," I do my best to see it into print. I knew placing the book with a publisher would not be difficult, given the freshness, the depth and intensity of the collection. In his last years, Morgan's poems were published individually and in groups in various journals as quickly as he could complete them.

Early on, Morgan faced the frustrations in publication of most young writers. But rejection of his work only energized his ambitions and intensified his discipline, just as setbacks in his medical condition made him work harder to stay well. He told me more than once that anger had been a motivating and creative emotion all his life, which always took me aback, given his charm and personable demeanor. Even in hospital, Morgan was determined to make the most of each day, often showering and dressing in street clothes before daylight and the first morning therapy so that he could work for a few hours before the next therapy—a schedule not that much different from his life outside the hospital. During those open seams of time each day, he culled words and phrases from, or found himself inspired by, his wide-ranging reading that included poetry and poetics, literary theory, politics and news, art and aesthetics, fiction, creative nonfiction and more. He filled numerous Moleskine notebooks with early drafts of poems and their scaffolding—words (often neologisms, or deliberate misspellings to create multiple meanings), phrases and ideas recorded in his meticulous and tiny print.

None of Morgan's family or friends had any expectation the surgery would not go well, once the lungs reached him. We fully anticipated more years of life, and many more poems, and we told him so. A soul and body more prepared for the rigors of transplant and recovery was hard to imagine. Morgan and I had a running argument—playful, but utterly serious—about who would die first. For years he'd been recognized by his doctors and nurses for his dedication, intensive therapies and personal discipline, staying as well as possible, given the inevitable damage cystic fibrosis would do to his lungs.

I met Morgan in the fall of 2000 when he entered the University of Arizona MFA program. We quickly became friends. By spring of 2002, he was already finding the music and conduct of language that would define the poems in his mature work. His innovation in language over the next few years—his dissection and remaking of words and memes—was astonishing to witness. Though I'd been his faculty mentor in the MFA program, working closely with him on the poems of his thesis, soon thereafter he became my most valued guide, directing my reading, challenging my assumptions about the very nature of poetry, and providing invaluable criticism of my work. I wasn't alone in receiving such gifts. He mentored many poets, in person and online, developing relationships and collaborating with writers throughout the country. A dedicated enthusiast of the work he loved, he co-founded and edited *CUE (A Journal of Prose Poetry)*, and edited *CUE* Editions, a chapbook series. During this period, he also wrote criticism, reviews and interviews, and maintained a lively blog.

I had no idea for some time the challenges Morgan faced medically. His lungs, unlike those of healthy people, did not have the ability to clear the moisture that builds up naturally as one breathes. He rarely mentioned the endless cycles of drugs and physical therapy. How could someone who looked so vital, someone so passionate and productive, be so sick? He would not be defined by the disease, he told me when I got to know him better. Eventually I witnessed the various procedures he undertook several times daily, the rounds of antibiotics, often inhaled, to hold infections in check, the vibrating vest and hand-held quake he employed to shake loose the mucous so that he could force-cough it out.

Morgan met—and surpassed—a set of ambitious educational and professional goals he set for himself in his late teens and twenties. A graduate of the University of Virginia, Charlottesville, where he earned a BA in English, he completed an MFA in Poetry and an MA in Literature at the University of Arizona. His first book-length collection, *Verge*, was published by Parlor Press in 2007. Between 2007 and 2012 he also published three poetry chapbooks.

As his hospitalizations became more frequent and lengthy the last three years of his life, the scarring in the lungs limiting his ability to breathe and hold off infections, Morgan began to think of the poems he was writing for *Erros* as possibly his last chance to make an enduring contribution to American poetry. He withdrew from the doctoral program at Arizona, gave up his college teaching, and concentrated on staying well enough to complete the extraordinary poems you will read here in this, his final collection.

—Boyer Rickel

erros

Desire that hollows us out and hollows us out,
That kills us and kills us and raises us up and
Raises us up.

—*Robert Hass*

That the syllables!

—*Ronald Johnson*

Disjecta Membra

When a man was unstrung from the gibbet, the students assembled in the gallery.

The surgeons gathered their various scalpels—trepans, rasps, lancets—and the cathedra was set above the bench where the body lay naked.

The physician—impeccably dressed in hat and gown—presided.

Because there was no preserving what was once begun, they worked outside by sun or torchlight. Four days, four nights.

To handle and to coax. Incise and unfasten. To disarticulate, without grace or technique, the most perishable parts first.

To sort past fat and sinew and viscera and to tend the red mess of the belly, the ligature of the neck and the head, the stiff- spun corded bundles of muscles in the arms and legs.

Four days and nights.

Prying at what's woven in.

Fingering and re-fingering a distinction.

Spreading it out piece by piece into a freedom the living know nothing of.

&

Residuary

Bc the bodye—
lopsed,   scrawned,   convolved—

is ex-why.
As gape, is ex-thrall.

Bc the bodye—
so dullable,   so diminished—

is attentions—
the sweet steady stabwork

through layer-names—
                              schema's

stratal *rather*
for what's

a slabbish slopping ago-thing.

Rack-lines & rank-mess.
Raw-red lapidaria
                    & redder dense

resistlessly skinned over
(w/ dayskin,   w/ nightskin).

Bc bodye is
gentleness
          when rinsed to see

the blode's rote under-runs.
Its skeins & valves

for O's efferent momentums.

Pinktricate deeps
            put to grind,

overwhelming their cause
(as willingness & unwillingness)

over who else is belonged to.

Bc *bodye*—
no ampling word—

dims into grammar.

Is cubic contents dead-ending
at intending,
            but as *intend*

love   (at least)
of being tried.

Bc bodye's the affliction.

An otherbody
            vivid

out of knowwhere slowing.

A quick & brink we become
accompanied w/.

Lung ache. *Lang-* ache.

(What's prone
            stranded

in mapblack in subreds.)

            My Indicatives,

when desire is *weak be over, be done,*

it will have seemd right
in this Unglish

to mean   to outlust.

Song Of The Idiot Bulk

This somewhat song.
From light to what's left,

may I dulge it?
-*ing*uistically?

In the last of the light,
the disassembling light

(ruin-yellow blew),
may I sing them—

this duskguise,
this strew-dark.

Oxygen
(its sweet knees),

& in silm
mutely.

Of this mouth,
that little *open*

(winning soft,
occupliable),

enjoying *upclose*,
or coming

(shakesbelieve)
to *try*, its angles.

Showmoving song
of salted greenshine

(waves, flash-jointed
plunges, runs)—

may I sing it?
From night to what's left

of this brunt's untaught
soft esoteries.

Its whole helve
& swelltips;

its betworks
& keepings;

a feeling of if
thrilled loose,

& its every
small prone

(in noiselets
as vigories).

Sung as if
sayparate.

Mademost,
madeleast

of light
& what's heft—

the mind,
that kinking

topknot
where it is

blood to remember.
How

as shirtsgo
haste

language is
strangelets.

Ambigracious.
First enough.

sPacific Ode

Overopposides—
an underlit   down-roar   rawther.

Whelmes   (more or restless
of *re-*, of *de-*)

soon't
ankle-deep answerable.

Thistinctions   this
                            too-do

end of June:
tilt-masts & sails   somehow
                                anyhow

swung & high. Less vivident—

that smooth middle   proof,

this sink-a-think
                        plunge, these

    high interiors of the se[e]   .

Vaults-chant quiet.

Underrupting.

Extantsy (Or The Long Night In Phrase)

The mere existence of emphasis—
a tramp   O   line   .

O   (that 'ccurs)—
lust's fed focus for the

little louds
        & outs

of yore's
on-and-on eloqwhence.

Nounsense for this   sprent
this stelléd   *else*—

disgathering night (its bulk

          flicker-heavied).

While succinct succulents
(salting down, ~~green~~)
          teem as *lean*.

While—wike awade—we tend to
meaning to

too neateningly.

To language
       & its many sudden lives.

       As if we could make
       —& w/ out awe—

the long night in a phrase.

Sounding
noose-rose & *wormfence.*

Sounding
fathomsuns & *shivelight.*

A l=u=n=g=u=a=g=e

violable—
hollow-bright.

Little Just Ones

My latest found , my sakesbelieve,
this nakeshift is—
our ownly
l=u=n=g=u=a=g=e.

Know apologeyesing.

This mincethrill voice
is yore's—

saysongs
metandmorefussed

in two's
& free's

of nonce-sense
phonicating.

Tremblestars—

dead *whens*
in the ever-during

dark

over us
so over -ous

)

Moreover,
     the moon.

Weflecting
     on its duskguise—

coeurious,
     amourtell.

Remember doing
andstands

under a vast etceterra
of aim-blue skigh

ends up ending
                    ?

Isn't it re-mantic,
mon share,
            how *now*

means

we once was others'
why's ?

(. . . *sick-tock*
        [sic]-talk . . .)

kiss'oclock in the mournin'—

· our   barebodied   bask about   bedst

& the sun
                        noone-due

at once   at twice
mmmemory . . .

Luke-summer
thaw-breeze—
                    sumthing

mouth-colored,
roamembered

suntinuing
as -*ous*

rehind kiss-lids
& thunkfully

O envything—

think-skinned, *I* lacks
alone in seeclusion.

Only these   seize-ons,
this whether,

& even these—
                    into thin err

My darling once,

barefully, skinsistently,

I phonesse
                    the limbits

&

The Mortician On The Act of
Seeing With One's Own Eyes

What is a bodye deprived
of adjectives?
                    Soulipsism?
          Skimatics?

Laved, loosed, letulled—

Airhow unasked for,
limited
          to unremembering.

An unexceptionable *in*
in which the packed
                    pieces
          abide?

Poem For Bob Flanagan

For envyone's clean-cornered envything—

you, in flesh in copes cared for,

wanting that thought
                    thought all—
that the body is a punishable place

to be beautiful in.

And from your side of portion.

From shouldhurry & the clairvoyance
of lusting roughly,

which is to say as mutualist, as agonal

in the pinks of condition
& bloodsummed.

A char-saint *before*

wanting more of *now &now*
                    & *not enough.*

Of pulver, of cram—
the *more* that racks museumly.

If brutals is pleasing means durance,
what much more of us is theirs?

Under-muscled, rushed.

Matter we have no choice in.

If bares is botch as irrangements of withins,
what & how avow?—

that pains is savors
                    is life
                              is refusings
            is life you most
                        imagined lasting?

Body As Go, Body As Believer

In lure-dark   as luxe functions
(chestfallsdeeply   darlingfondles)

loosening to be vocables to be vividry to be
sweet unpack
                    oversufficience & *slow*

that part of expectations
that is night-sourced   that is black-breakingly beautiful—

innovationless dark
loved by more than one

mouth   full of mentions
of how description
                    comes to an end somewhere

how anything above enough
freezes or burns

how if it were body as go
as believer

the pain
wd be with & w/ out form

                    usefulness longing

for how nothing in a word

(other than us)
                    performs

The Mortician's Little Deathling
On Being Prone

My beautiful *beforehand*—
               decrep
                           painted wide.
My midsting handscapes—
                 weren't they

showmantic . . .
            Land-roughed, air-toughed
                                 something
thigh here now, something
                 thinlet, your

dim-lit mingle, your true.

Grudgework
            glozed; blinkhard
                     loverhood
untroublously strew:
                zipper-shriven.
                         You?

Homage To Francis Bacon I

Criss-couple
  crosse-messed.

Pulverous
  the postures. Grim-

matical touchlines
co-here-ing
  as bash.

Big moreboys in pumps   at knot.

  Flung-fucked. Fragile.

Bald-bright
in the afterdamp.

Semi-sided—
      peenings,
  un-pent,

      ↙
the bodies' rote riggings

blood-dumb-suddenly

  loosed. Violence

its own destined   -ation.

Desire—
    hack-deep; pinks

&   casual.

Plainsong (For One)

Plays attentions.
Plays bides

& goes weak
w/ another's

ponderable
body.

Plays emphas,
plays *is*.

Catapult
& condoles.

Luke-sick
& sweaty

w/ boundary

(vivident
volving verge),

plays sometimes boil
to others

on mess-sheets

taking
a long dying

often time.
Each draw,

each repeat
plays speculations.

Ardors—
the randoms grim.

Appetitive. Debauch.

Hale
'gainst ex-

& lossly
when ruining too

easy.
When underdying,

under-intentioned.
Plays the stills

consecutively.
W/ out complining.

Poem For Emerson

Dying of miscellany.

Lungs billow-pink for something resemblable—

the unassemblable suddening
                    all-sorts-of-befores.

Dunes weighting & re-weighting
w/ *this & that.*

Waves' booming seams ramping
                    & reramping—

(as suck & sough & hish & __)—

somethingth
tending _____-ly away

(some   where   else   where.)

From what set-asides, My Optative,
My *–Eth,*

does this throwback shockwork dote?

Amid this unstructing copia,
thru surround & resurround
                    & from inskied out—

throes are throughs
          & there is no mattering
that is not ours.
                    Hours

when sake's done most
enough,   taken for holdable.

As lustrations.

As meatpack in fuckery—

the blood's hectivities
when *we* is not   gently.

But sound-sided;

choicelessly
              skinsideout.

Though shareful for being so.

The Mortician On Palimprest

Even you, starveling dulling.
The heat hangs in you

as seep
so that, un-hesive,

the slack skin set afloat
in places   in pieces
                    unsingles.

&

Plainsong (For Two)

Botch or not,
this body

(so troped for)—
how hapless

& hand-to-mouth
each day has it.

Botch or not (or
mess of fix),

how, marrow-casually,
you'll've

loved it
most. Its lasting.

Its ravel-song
sung thew—O

butcher reds,
O offal proof

! This
descript *despite,*

a half-riddance
slowing, now,

from purpose.
Slowing *how*

to dististances

(up |room |
| down | room).

The *lent* relenting
merely to relate

merely.

Linen-long.
Under scar-lights.

Homage To Francis Bacon II

Pinks
       sounding down

to slick-noise. Rough-through

w/ man-alive private.

Vowels   (hurrious

as blurs)
            side-wise tangled—

       so much of a skinful mingled
abrupt.

Jounced. Flensed. Gangled.

Throughent:
       how lust makes

    ↙
ends meat;

how meat sakes *meta-*.

Rescindence

What lasts   come after decades
hands' approaches?

                When the interdarks'
cordoned gores

listlessen   crescend   & want

is a room waves make move
no psalt
        can preserve or keep

preserve or keep.
                This situation of meat,
this cut-short shut of mess stairs-slow—

in scants of fantasts   fears fucking;
it makes no promises back.

O *Thenatos,*
even in its sensefulness of night & day

(years of hours of attentions
languaged w/ openings)

the sky always an *a*'s shade of blue
like skin
        the *a*'s shade of blue I cannot believe

my way out of.

Or whether we cld *we*—
what's breathed about

& how the mouth makes boundaries
                hands test

again,
        tending & re-tending
w/ the eloquence of blood-rush.

Becoming Regardless

Days giving way like birthbone.

Days blanded *and*.
                    (Atlas atless   at last.)

Days custodial whites.
Ex-colored.   Hip-strange.

Days lettering go,
decompounding from the darling

misbehaviors
            of *did-we-dare?*

Thy everyone's lovely *down* thus—

jealous assemblies
                   waned groundward

from rush & gush & too much emphasis.

From bell-pull lusts burning out
                              at one another

& the milkblue body,
tight by tight,
               worth destroyings.

Unhanced faux betweens
roughed so skinningly,

roughing, now, so skinnyingly.
again^st *un*ishments.

(The pacenotes, the flexion,
even dumbly in their being pent.)

                    If I could forget
this breatheathing.

Forget the handholds
—these *and*holds—
                    of the ribcage

& whateverelse
light
does outside us.

Memento Mori

O   bright confines

—Ronald Johnson

Like the heard words in the sounds—
every place we are
                    is one we'll aren't.
Elaboratably.

So, over-and-over.   So arterialy.

    (Re-occasion's slow abrade.)

As in—*these rawing err-ways breach bloud mash-barrel reds.*

Trace.   Afrer-scapes.

As in—this dimming makes meaning make
more sense   on the inhale.

Like dusk in the olde adjectives,

these plush, rushed _-teriors
(courses sorted,
                    under-messed). Words

unchanging long and long

—lust's mince gears.

    (Stripped.)

Nightish musclings—
                    wine-deep.
        But speeded.

Hands skim-wilde
on the gathering side

as mingle   as outdulge

where lies kindly   distract
from the sick-spoon

from the lunks' jungs
                        & our skin (spikeless

twinlipspink)—
            their throughency

cramming bare whereabouts
(the oceanwork dark)

w/ howabouts
            as if *diminish*

meant
        (should mean)

where the white halts loft
                    to steeps
                            to break

(as vanish, unespecially)
the jetties' black angles into sands.

Aubade

Waking to *must*, there are those who want
to bruise
        in god's hands.

On eye-catch, eye-volved
                memorial distances

      —(rule-half, half water)—
                    they brood.

But where sound opens
zound, where   *up*   breaks sibilant,

where coastwise
           fadings fold   & open-
                    air-suddenly

all tenses are born
                 a dead-bless
   -scending   pull
            on the body—
     a body

(nakeshift & brine-slung,
wet-greened
        & pleas'd),

        built for resistence
among the waves.

Hear his pent bulk
        singing: O

    scatter! O idiot rummage!

Here hymnself

                    junelooking
for clear lacknowledgements

which are

allmost 'causes—

                  Omost causes. Their

immense grammaries.

&

Re-mantic CentO^{de}

O air,
O death, sole kiss for silenced mouths unfed,
O wester wind let's not.
O the mind, mind has mountains, cliffs of fall
shaped by teeth O with O the letter O a howl
and O, I am afraid!   Our love has red in it   and
A black, E white, I red, O blue, U green—
O what a physical effect it has on me
in my life O this life. Yes, this one. O, it!
O, to release the first music somewhere again, for a moment,
o'er the disordered scenes of woods and fields,
o'er evening hills they glimmer; and I knew
"I FELL IN LOVE." O none of this foreseen.

                        O reader of the future,
listen to the night as it makes itself hollow. O stars
your power, like a language of whiteness, O Ocean.
O one, O none, O nobody, you,
O Walt!—ascensions of thee hover in me now.
O ruddy god in our veins, O fiery god in our genitals,
O speak of not enough.
O enter an apostrophe
to blaze   O the bring of blood
into new bodies: O gods above, inspire
(-ologies be damned)
an interminable list of romantic O's.
O verb, O void,
O evidence of blood—
O, for a Life of Sensation!
Darkness, O Father of Charity, lay on your hands.
Make me, O Lord, a last, a simple thing,
op'ning the soul's most subtle rooms.
And O that awful deepdown torrent O and the sea the sea crimson,
O diver, to be sea-surrounded by a thought bled white—a blank-
    ness as likely as blackness.

O we waited so long in the waves.)

Then O, through the underwater time of night—
O. O. O. The libertine bell.
You give, O lips, the supreme tortured moans.
O give me burning blue!
O help me through the fact of you, unfasten
O Eros, mangier than I, the nervous coils.

Send our delicately scented innards our O so small

presence O—
                O, let me suffer, being at your beck.
O fluent one, O muscle full of hydrogen,
O now no longer speak,   but rather seem.
O laugh it out roundlaughingly, the laugh of laughed-at laughians!

And this:? < O
O caring and not caring outside me quiet,
turn us again, O,
to the O's collapse
and sighing. These lives are not your lives, O free,
O desire reclining.
                        O heart whose beating blood was running song,
blowing, blissful, open. O most immaculate bleached
of speed. O limit case. Why linger?
The beach ignores the power of words as words ignore the power of things O stranger
behind me. O world that forces joy,
no is the O, the concentric; how to open the O, undo the easy-for-me round of renounc
                                                O causes,
                                O certainties,
                        O, vestiges that limit us, O, vast machinery of what—
call it a night.   O soul.   Flow on.   Instead

Notes

"Residuary" is for Charles Wright.

"sPacific Ode" transposes a letter from the phrase "high interiors of the sea," which originally appears in Herman Melville's *Moby Dick*. The poem is dedicated to Barbara Cully.

The italicized line in "Song Of The Idiot Bulk" is lifted from William James.

In the poem "Extantsy (Or The Long Night In Phrase)," the wording "The mere existence of emphasis" is from Frank O'Hara's poem "In Memory of My Feelings." The poem also borrows the following: "wormfence" from Walt Whitman; "fathomsuns" from Paul Celan; and "shivelight" from Gerard Manley Hopkins.

"The Mortician On The Act Of Seeing With One's Own Eyes" was inspired by Stan Brakhage's documentary *The Act of Seeing With One's Own Eyes*. The poem is dedicated to Lisa Jarnot who recommended the film.

"Poem For Emerson" borrows the phrase "dying of miscellany" from the journals of Ralph Waldo Emerson.

"Homage To Bob Flanagan" was written for the writer, performance artist, and self-described "supermasochist." His struggle with— and subsequent death from—cystic fibrosis are chronicled in Kirby Dick's documentary *Sick*.

In the poem "Rescindence," the phrase "this situation of meat" is attributable to the painter, Francis Bacon; it is dedicated to Boyer Rickel.

"Becoming Regardless" is for Cristina Maldonado.

The phrase "unchanging long and long" in the poem "Memento Mori" is borrowed from Walt Whitman.

"Re-mantic CentO^{de}" is built with lines—some altered for end-stop punctuation, some not—taken from the following poets in the following order: James Schuyler, Federico García Lorca, Peter Gizzi, Gerard Manley Hopkins, Christian Hawkey, Ted Berrigan, Arthur Rimbaud, Kenneth Koch, Rod Smith, Robert Duncan, John Clare, Percy Bysshe Shelley, John Berryman, Walt Whitman, Rainer Maria Rilke, Pablo Neruda, Paul Celan, Hart Crane, D.H. Lawrence, Andrew Zawacki, Christopher Rizzo, Alex Lemon, Ovid, Morgan Lucas Schuldt, Matt Hart, Karen Volkman, Allison Titus, John Keats, Charles Wright, Theodore Roethke, George Herbert, James Joyce, Andrew Joron, Frank Stanford, Jack Gilbert, Anne Boyer, Stéphane Mallarmé, H.D., Joshua Kryah, Lisa Jarnot, Olena Kalytiak Davis, S.A. Stepanek, William Shakespeare, Heather McHugh, John Ashbery, Velimir Khlebnikov, Kristi Maxwell, Matthew Zapruder, Robert Johnson, Dan Beachy-Quick, Wallace Stevens, Barbara Cully, A.C. Swinburne, Harryette Mullen, Kiki Petrosino, Lisa Russ Spaar, G.C. Waldrep, Liz Waldner, Barbara Guest, Frank O'Hara, Nate Pritts, C.D. Wright.

Acknowledgments

American Letters & Commentary: "Body As Go, Body As Believer"
The Benefactor: "Poem For Bob Flanagan"
Coconut: "sPacific Ode" and "Aubade"
EOAGH: "Song Of The Idiot Bulk" and "Plainsong (For One)"
The Equalizer: "The Mortician On The Act of Seeing With One's Own Eyes," "Poem For Emerson," and "Homage To Francis Bacon II"
Fou: "Memento Mori"
Free Verse: "Extantsy (Or The Long Nights In Phrase)," "Plainsong (For Two)," "Rescindence," and "Residuary" (poems first published in the chapbook *(as vanash, unespecially))*
Gondola: "Little Just Ones"
H_NGM_N: "The Mortician's Little Deathling On Being Prone" and "The Mortician On Palimprest"
Phoebe: "Disjecta Membra"
Tight: "Homage To Francis Bacon I"
Transom: "Re-mantic CentO^{de}"

The poem "Becoming Regardless" first appeared as a pamphlet with Greying Ghost Press.

Thanks to Scantily Clad Press for publishing a portion of these poems in the online chapbook *L=u=N=G=U=A=G=E* and to Sommer Browning and Tony Mancus at Flying Guillotine Press for the care they showed in publishing the chapbook *(as vanish, unespecially)*.

About the Author

Morgan Lucas Schuldt died of complications from cystic fibrosis on Jan. 30, 2012, twelve days before his thirty-fourth birthday. Schuldt earned an MFA in Poetry and an MA in Literature at the University of Arizona. He completed two book-length collections, *Erros* and *Verge* (Parlor Press, 2007), as well as three chapbooks, *(as vanish, unespecially)* (Flying Guillotine Press, 2012), *L=u=N=G=U=A=G=E* (Scantily Clad Press, 2009) and *Otherhow* (Kitchen Press, 2007). A writer of criticism, reviews and interviews, he was a mentor to many poets and a dedicated enthusiast of the work he loved, co-founding and editing *CUE* (A Journal of Prose Poetry), and editing *CUE* Editions, a chapbook series.

Photograph of Morgan Lucas Schuldt by
Barbara Cully. Used by permission.

Free Verse Editions

Edited by Jon Thompson

13 ways of happily by Emily Carr
Between the Twilight and the Sky by Jennie Neighbors
Blood Orbits by Ger Killeen
The Bodies by Chris Sindt
The Book of Isaac by Aidan Semmens
Canticle of the Night Path by Jennifer Atkinson
Child in the Road by Cindy Savett
Contrapuntal by Christopher Kondrich
Country Album by James Capozzi
The Curiosities by Brittany Perham
Current by Lisa Fishman
Divination Machine by F. Daniel Rzicznek
Erros by Morgan Lucas Schuldt
The Forever Notes by Ethel Rackin
The Flying House by Dawn-Michelle Baude
Instances: Selected Poems by Jeongrye Choi, translated by Brenda Hill-
    man, Wayne de Fremery, and Jeongrye Choi
A Map of Faring by Peter Riley
Physis by Nicolas Pesque, translated by Cole Swensen
Poems from above the Hill & Selected Work by Ashur Etwebi, translated
    by Brenda Hillman and Diallah Haidar
The Prison Poems by Miguel Hernández, translated by Michael Smith
Puppet Wardrobe by Daniel Tiffany
Quarry by Carolyn Guinzio
remanence by Boyer Rickel
Signs Following by Ger Killeen
These Beautiful Limits by Thomas Lisk
An Unchanging Blue: Selected Poems 1962–1975 by Rolf Dieter Brink-
    mann, translated by Mark Terrill
Under the Quick by Molly Bendall
Verge by Morgan Lucas Schuldt
The Wash by Adam Clay
We'll See by George Godeau, translated by Kathleen McGookey
What Stillness Illuminated by Yermiyahu Ahron Taub
Winter Journey [Viaggio d'inverno] by Attilio Bertolucci, translated by
    Nicholas Benson

www.ingramcontent.com/pod-product-compliance
Lightning Source LLC
Chambersburg PA
CBHW022039090426

42741CB00007B/1133

9781602353763